Wayfaring

Liza Hyatt

Fernwood
PRESS

Wayfaring

©2024 by Liza Hyatt

Fernwood Press
Newberg, Oregon
www.fernwoodpress.com

Printed in the United States of America

Cover and page design: Mareesa Fawver Moss
Cover photo: Eric Muhr, www.ericmuhr.photo

ISBN 978-1-59498-124-1

Dedicated

to Jan Lundy and Jeanette Banashak, wise guides, teachers, and founders of the Spiritual Guidance Training Institute—

and my fellow pilgrims there: Kitty, Cathy, Matt, Eric, Robin, Rose, Allyssa—

to Mary Jo and Roger and all the Natural Dreamwork team, who honor the sacred presence and healing within our dreams—

to all my art therapy colleagues and students from whom I am always learning to respond to the world with courageous, compassionate creativity—

to Sandra, Francis, Bev, Judy, Norbert, Katherine, Mary Lou, and Ruth—trusted companions on the spiritual path—

and to Maggie and Gary, who encourage me to wander and wonder—

wayfaring with each of you has changed my life for the better forever.

Contents

Acknowledgments

"Simple Walking Meditation" and "Sitting in My Car in a
Rural Indiana Parking Lot" were published in *Buddhist
Poetry Review*, Volume 2, Issue 1, Summer 2015.

"At St. Joseph's Lake in April" was published in *Branches
Magazine: Best Medicine*—Volume 26, No. 2, May–June 2013.

"Meditation on the Word *Through*" was published in *Branches
Magazine: Grace*—Volume 26, No. 5, November–December
2013.

"Decrescendo" was published in *Last Stanza Poetry Journal:
Altered States*, Issue 3, January 2021.

A stanza of "Home Song" was included in *Family Celebrations:
Poems, Toasts, and Traditions for Every Occasion*, editors
June Cotner and Nancy Tupper Ling, Andrews McMeel
Publishing: Kansas City, MO, 2018.

"Song" and "Sacred Words in Sacred Places" were published in
*Laureate—The Literary Journal of Arts for Lawrence: Grand
Opening*, Issue 1, May 2021.

"We Are All On a Boat" was selected in June 2021 for inclusion in the *INverse Poetry Archive* (found at https://indianamemory.contentdm.oclc.org/digital/collection/p16066coll82/search), a collaborative online collection of poetry by Indiana poets maintained by the Indiana Arts Commission and the Indiana State Library.

"Song" was published in *The Minimum Wager*, Issue No. 7, January 2022.

"Commute Home" was published in *The Minimum Wager*, Issue No. 8, March, 2022.

"We Are All On a Boat" was published in *The Minimum Wager*, Issue No. 10, July 2022.

We have to find a way to reconnect with what is essential—to learn once again how to walk in a sacred manner, how to breathe with awareness, cook with love and prayers, how to give attention to simple things. We need to learn to welcome life in all its colors and fragrances, to say "yes" again and again. Then life will give us back our connection to our own soul, and once more we will hear its song.

—Llewellyn Vaughan-Lee
(*Spiritual Ecology: 10 Practices to Reawaken the Sacred in Everyday Life*, pg. 90–91)

Introduction:

From One Wayfarer to Another

"And it was at that age, poetry arrived in search of me"
—Pablo Neruda

A wayfarer is a spiritual seeker who does not withdraw from the world but lives compassionately within it, attuning the heart to open to the sacred in every moment, every thing, and every interaction. Through wayfaring, the seeker becomes a poet. To speak of sacred encounter, language steeped in awe is brought to the edge of silence. Poetry is an attuning practice of deep listening, of opening one's heart, of only speaking when each word is one of reverence and restraint. While creating poetry, the poet is wayfaring; when walking the world with open heart, the wayfarer experiences life's poetry and grows ever more capable of opening to the sacred in the smallest, most ordinary of moments. Wayfaring makes the seeker a poet; writing poetry makes her a wayfarer.

As the author of this collection of poems, I can't remember a time before I was wayfarer or poet. Surely, I was born wayfaring. Just as surely, I was born a poet. When I trace back through my years, I see at every age poetry arriving in search of me—the toddler mesmerized by rhymes; the second grader encouraged to sit on the grass and write about clouds; the grown woman who has come to trust the soul's imagination, depth, and numinous vision, who remains as eager as a child to give voice to this awe.

Being born poet and wayfarer means being born human. These callings are not special or elite. They belong to us all and reside deeply in us, the birthright of body and soul. Each of us is born from the *poiesis* of the universe—the creative energy of making and being transformed within the making. So, nothing can completely sever us from this sacred poetry. The trauma, oppression, and spiritual injury we suffer may quiet the poetic soul within us, but it is never lost. It can be always rediscovered and, from its wellsprings, bathe us in healing song.

To rediscover our inherent belonging to creation's sacred poetry, we need simple practices, daily rituals that help us reconnect, root back into the realness of life, and return to our embodied belonging in the world's wild relational web. The simpler the practice the better. Esoteric, complicated, hard-to-maintain spiritual practices are not necessary and are too punishing. Instead, opening one's heart and being awake and present amidst what one already does, day after day, allows every moment to become healing ground. Sitting at the window, driving the morning commute, walking the dog, listening to another's story, breathing, dreaming, chopping vegetables, adding salt to the broth, asking a question—each ordinary repeated gesture of a day becomes loving practice in reconnecting to life.

These poems are offered in trust that you, the reader, come to them in some need of healing while yet also knowing yourself as a fellow poet and wayfarer, somewhere on the path of rediscovering the abundant sacred poetry within your life. These poems trust that you too have experienced one or more moments in which the wild love that births this universe broke through to your heart and revealed the sacred in the simplest of things.

These poems are born from my daily life, from all the little ways I routinely seek and find deep belonging. These poems come from humble, human, common spaces, where our paths cross, hiking trails and sidewalks, highways and local streets, gardens, kitchens, soup kettles, porch chairs, dreamscapes, and places of sorrow and struggle. May my poetry bless and enliven your daily journeys through marketplace and home, through pain and joy. May my poetry help you hear your own soul-songs of deep longing and real epiphanies that burst forth while folding the laundry or crossing the street where you live. May my poems nourish the wayfarer in you so that, wherever you go, poetry arrives in search of you, with every step and every breath you take.

Walking

Simple Walking Meditation

From one step
to the next,
I go from
not awake
to awake.

From one breath
to the next,
I go from
empty and alone
to full and with.

From one thought
to the next,
I go from
"I have failed—"
to "Such beauty!"

Moon Sliver

The dark side of the moon
sits in the light side's silver chalice
like a wine of sea-blue grapes
or a loaf of granite-ground grain.

A thin haze of clouds slowly covers them
like a priest placing a gossamer cloth.

This morning has been consecrated.

I walk home, rejoicing.
For the rest of the day,
what we do, say, and share
will be communion.

How I take the garbage out.
How the garbage men collect it.

The steeping of tea.

This poem I am now writing.
All the words that will be spoken.

Each note of music played.

And all the ways we
recognize and tend
each other's needs.

Tikkun Olam*

While walking down a busy street
I've never walked before,
a sign outside a synagogue invites:
LET'S REPAIR THE WORLD TOGETHER

to which my weariness responds:
"This world is irreparably broken."

And so? some part of my heart still asks—

and is answered immediately
by a response that feels
here all along
inside everything,
the synagogue, apartment buildings,
school, hospital, street, sidewalk,
ground, and sky:
>   *And so, there are endless possibilities of repair,*
>   *endless opportunities to repair.*

"But *I* am forever broken," I offer.

>   *And so*—comes the response—
>   *forever healing,*
>   *forever*
>   *healing.*

Shame evaporates.
Shame and the hiding
from shame evaporate.

I walk along,
one of the broken people
born of this broken, healing world.

The sidewalk is crowded with strangers—
old people, young people,
parents pushing strollers,
dogs, babies.
I love us all.

*a Jewish concept meaning repair of the world

At St. Joseph's Lake in April

Six turtles sun themselves
on a log in the lake:
breath and a slight turn of the head.

The ballooning song of frogs:
open the throat and huge sound
rolls from small bodies.

Trees sway in the wind,
and the wind plays their reflections:
vibrating strings, marbled paper.

The wind itself: vibrations
of sun warmth, sea currents, earth spin.
Nothing forced. Flowing through stillness. Carried along.

The turkey vulture, looping in swift circles,
isn't moving, just holds still
and lets the wind carry it.

Even the geese swimming by
push only enough to allow
the lake's gentlest waves
to carry them forward.

Everything is carried. Everything is supported.
Everything makes the least effort in its body.
And is set free.

May Journey

Needing to be together more deeply,
we left home and wandered north
until we returned to spring.

We found a trail of painted trillium
and hiked to the waterfall
over which moosewood viburnum
held restrained and wide-open flowers.

We hiked to the summit
and met others walking the spine
of the old mother mountains,
going north, going south,
on long memories of stone,
pine needle, rain, wind,
sun, and deerskin moccasin.

We watched a hawk and eagle,
circling, chasing each other.

We felt layers of false-self
loosen and fall away.
Everyone we met
knew why this is necessary,
for them, for us.

When we returned,
home was truly home.

We woke in the morning,
knowing we had been
too long afraid of more loss.
We woke knowing our hearts
will open into Great Spirit
now that they are opening.

First Steps of the Day

The pink late-summer roses
and the rose-gold early morning sky
create each other,
dwell in each other's skin,
and dream each other's dreams.

Waking, taking first steps of the day,
we can all know this,
all feel it.
The rabbit, alert in the grass.
The bath-robed newspaper seeker.
The dog walkers.

To say everything is connected
doesn't say enough.
Intimate.
Utterly intimate
and right now, climaxing.

Every wet cell. Every subatomic blush.
Knows each other.
Comes to be
inside each other.

Blossoming inside blossoming
inside blossoming inside blossoming
inside blossoming.

Lunch Break with the Muse

Put on the sneakers kept under your desk
and head to the paths around the pond
and through undeveloped fields
between corporate office buildings.

There will be tropical humidity,
an August noon,
cloud mountains gathering evening rain,
crickets and grasshoppers,
a little green heron in shallow water,
yellow-petalled prairie flowers,
grasses gone to seed,
the smell of all this steeping in the sun,
few shadows, tepid shade,
sweat dripping down the spine,
a hawk high in a thermal updraft,
a day meant for swimming.

And so, as your middle-aged body
reluctantly walks
the simmering sidewalk
back to work,
dive into the memories
given to you for life by your child-self
and swim in the cold expanse
of the small-town swimming pool,
doing frog kicks and mermaid glides,
long hair flowing under turquoise water.

What I Carry Home with Me

Wet stones from the middle path.

A shard of green heartwood

ripped by the big storm

from the oak's broken, heavy limb.

And we all have scar stories.

Which say more than wound stories.

Wound stories tell how we were injured.

Scar stories tell how we heal.

Having Come upon an Uprooted Old Tree

When this old tree fell in the forest,
it bent down saplings
that grew from its seeds.

Nothing can stop this.
We will shoulder
our parents' grief,

and it will weigh on us
and be ours to carry,
even as we keep growing.

Migration

I step outside into the call
of sandhill cranes, rippling
in the high currents.

I walk, looking up, turning in all directions,
shielding my eyes from the sun
like someone lost in a wilderness,
looking for the helicopter they hear
and need to rescue them.

I search with longing
for the high-flying flock,
but everywhere I turn,
I see empty sky and stand bereft.

Then I see it, one bird
separated from its group,
calling and being answered,
finding its way back
to others unseen.

I flew solo for so long,
pretending I was strong.
Now I'm relearning
homing instincts
for belonging.
This ache shapes my life
the way water softens rock,
the way wind currents make the flyway.

Christmas Morning

As if sensing this is a day for gifts,
the dog insists we walk
a way we never go,
discovering a scent hidden under
new snow dusting the sidewalk,
glittering like the path of a star,
which she tracks with her nose.

The tipped half-moon
is a silver ladle
pouring out sunrise
the color of honey and cider,
wassail brewed in the sky,
departing winter storm
afire with dawn.

Midlife Love

Today, out walking,
from my ordinary house
through my ordinary neighborhood,
I stop in my tracks, hand on heart,
making peace,
finding courage,
suddenly able to accept, that, yes,
I will never have
the house, job, spouse
of my dreams.

Instead of defeat, joy.

I am free.

From now on,
I get to love
all the other
imperfect people

often
and imperfectly.

Driving

Commute Home

The audiobook is talking about
the disappointment of the early Christians,
waiting and waiting for the transformation
they believed would happen
in their lifetime
until they grew to find
eternity and salvation
inside the waiting
as waiting changed them,
teaching them
to love each other.

A livestock semitrailer
is slowly passing me.
Pushed into each oval air-hole,
black and white fur of cows
packed in for a long journey.
From one of these holes,
a single, velvet cow ear,
flapping in the winter air.

I long to reach out
and touch its softness;
I feel sudden tenderness
for these animals
and their life of sacrifice.

I arrive home
less disappointed in marriage,
practicing the faith born
from knowing we
failed and fail and will fail,
yet continue to choose
a forgiving love
with which we redeem
each other.

Real and Imagined Streets I've Traveled

Easy Street—full of potholes.

Hoard Avenue—the entrance to a suburban shopping mall.

Faith Street—not the dead end I feared.

A country road whose name changes from Long to Winding.

In one neighborhood, still under construction:
Liberation Drive. Bliss Street. Tao Way.
Here Court and Now Court—both cul-de-sacs.

And I live at the intersection of
Long-Lost and Found-At-Last Lanes.

Come visit.

Talking to the World as I Drive at Dawn

Inside a bubble of car
as it floats on gray roads,
darkness changing to cloud-silver,

true words burrow out
from an opening in my heart,
and wisdom, until now hidden,

peeks out at the world
through my mouth,
warmed by my breath;

and that larger, wild,
ever-listening consciousness
to whom I speak

strongly senses my quiet voice,
my heart's subtle stirring,
and seizes joyfully

what I am praying, hungry
for it, enlivened by it,
just as the hawk

in the top branches of a tree
at the highway's edge
sees, hears the brief movement,

the faintest nibbling, and dives
straight toward its dawn meal,
the field mouse in the grass.

After Commuting 200,000 Miles in My 5th Car

At dawn, the day's first stoplight
has just turned green,
and someone two cars back
lays on the horn.

At dusk, as I put on the brake,
the truck tailgating me
guns into the open turn lane
and flies straight through
as the light turns red.

When this car was new, I felt still young,
in a hurry, driven by conflicting needs,
scrambling breakneck toward mirages.

But the current that slowly
draws us toward death's horizon
has pulled me miles from shore
into deep mid-sea waters.

Here, whatever I do,
no matter how urgently,
I seem to remain in place,
surrounded by the vast immeasurable,
overcome by this expanse.

Sometimes, frightened to be
so diminished, I fire up my engines,
insist I have it in me, should have it in me,
to start a second career, run a marathon,
win prestigious awards, get a Ph.D.

But then I hear it,
the voice that slows me,
that wells up from fecund nothingness
from the nourishing abyss:

Do you really need to keep feeding
those hungry ghosts?

Here and There, Now and Then

In thirty minutes, I easily drive
from my midlife house
to the house where I breathed
infant breaths,
but I can never get to
the beginning
or the end
of this journey.
Such places exist only in mind.

Rush Hour, First Week of March

We all suffer.
That woman walking
to the bus stop in a headwind.
That man weaving through lanes
without signaling.
All of us, somewhere between
new wound and healed wound.

What we feel is so complex,
we need simple words,
what friends say to each other,
space for listening,
absence of cleverness.

Be glad for unsettled days like today.
This transitioning between winter and spring.
The wind. Whirlpools of old brown leaves
and litter between curb and parking lot.
Everything that was dormant, now off balance.

In thick clouds, gray and luminous,
there is one clear circle of blue sky, opening,
sunbeams streaming through.

My heart leaps toward it
like I was in a deep, dark well
and finally see daylight and a rope.

Driving Mantra

In every car,
someone like me
hurrying to work,
hurrying home.

We arrive
where we need to be

as soon as
we help
each other.

Gardening and Cooking

Sparrows and Dandelions

Three brown sparrows
and many dandelions
gone to seed,
wet with rain.

Simple things, known all my life,
like shoestrings and crackers.
Yet, life half over,
I just now see:

sparrows eat dandelion seeds.

These three
flutter onto pliant stalks
to bend damp-haired heads to the grass,
beaks swallowing dewy fluff,
a morning's feast.

I now see,
finally,
these lives
are linked.

How little I know
about all the little things
I think I know,

every little thing
in relationship
with every other thing,

beginning right here
with these
small birds
and these
wildflowers.

Early Summer Evening

Mint grows between the strawberries,
and red-winged blackbirds sing
in the cattails on the bank of the pond.
The sun, tart red on the horizon's tongue,
sets behind the cherry tree.
All day long, it brewed the humid air
into sweet herb tea. Now, at dusk,
let's go to the garden,
pick berries, stir the steeped air
with sweat-sweetened bodies,
wet lips with berry juice,
then kiss and drink long draughts
of early summer's blood-warm potion.

Garden Meditation

A goldfinch comes
to feast on a sunflower
as a tiger swallowtail drifts by,
glowing in summer noon,
and amber bees embrace
the bristled, orange seed crowns
of the echinacea.

In this moment,
every living thing,
including me,
is able to find
and savor
such secret honey
infusing the world.

For the Oregano at Our Doorstep

All summer long, we cross
the front doorstep threshold
overgrown with oregano,
a low curtain of lavender flowers,
aroma of hillside, sun, and sea,
bees and butterflies,
a pair of mating whites,
dozens of red admirals,
the occasional great spangled fritillary.

Oh, rampant herb,
whose name means joy of the mountains,
lucky bounty of negligent gardening,
flowered wreath of Aphrodite,

may your household magic
steep us in a potion
of happiness, health, tranquility,

soothe, protect, and bring dreams,

work a spell of letting go
and deepening love,

until we pause
and feel what has been here always,
the breathing body's simple bliss,
buzzing inside breast and bone.

Slowing Until at Last

Full of self,
always some heavy,
round urgency
to push uphill,
with every pause for breath,
a harsh voice demands,
"Keep pushing!
Hurry! Work harder!
There is no time to feel."

Suddenly stopping,
lie on the ground
and watch the clouds,
the trees, the birds flowing,
and realize how open,
how quiet, how roomy
and unfamiliar
this body is.

The world welcomes you.

And the rock-hard, old
false-self careens unretrieved
down its rutted path
and out of sight
until it reaches a gentle
and complete stop.

A Bowl of Cherries

The half-dead, half-priced tree
planted the summer after my divorce,
ten-and-counting years ago,
filled my blue bowl this morning
with hundreds of red cherries.

All day, I am glad for this life.
Never the one we want.
Always the one that slowly sets us free.

All day, I take cherries from the bowl,
tasting the sour in the sweet,
tasting the sweet in the sour.

Being Cooked

I'm longer making do on tidbits.
Substantial love has melted—
like slow-churned butter,
like long-simmered lentil soup—
into every place, every relationship,
the daily bread that soaks love up.

This melting wasn't quick or easy.
Long, slow heat was required.
Deep below the surface,
a tenacious spark
insisted upon this cooking
through decades when
love felt impossible,
a birthright I was expelled from.

Life seemed a turbulent sea storm of
happenstance, accidents, and failures
with no home, only a leaky, battered boat.

But as I kept patiently seeking,
improvising from what life offered,
that spark transformed lack into blessing,
storm-silted water into wine,
dregs into stars,
the thin, stolen broth of survival
into a harvest's hearty chowder,
which I now savor.

Kitchen Prayer

For all those who are imperfect,
who break plates and spill wine and fail,
for all the rough shards that loss brings,
and all the rebuilding we do—
a wise mother's kitchen prayer:
bless *this* mess!

For bread dough, clogged sinks, and sorrow,
for deep hungers not easily fed,
for struggle, conflict, and longing,
for living life passionately—
a wise mother's kitchen prayer:
bless *this* mess!

For artists mixing wet colors
and children afire with wild play,
for grievers, seekers, and growers,
and those risking love's alchemy—
a wise mother's kitchen prayer:
bless *this* mess!

For the wounds we give each other
and the wounds we give living Earth,
for the tears that bring our healing,
for working to birth a new age—
a wise mother's kitchen prayer:
bless this mess!

Apprentice to Joy

Today, I wrote in the morning,
did gentle yoga, meditated,
then went to the forest and hiked
with my dog and my sweetheart.

I heard, then saw, sandhill cranes heading north.
I discovered the year's first wildflowers—
harbinger of spring, down near the creek,
and hepatica, high on the ridge.

I made blueberry buttermilk pancakes
and ate them for dinner.

Chopping Vegetables

This carrot is the sun's finger
materialized in soil.
These mushrooms are wet breaths of loam.
Each strip I cut from the red bell pepper
is the rough tongue of a wildcat lapping up blood.

When younger, I hungered
for more than is,
believed I would leave home and never come back.
Along the way, I have eaten thousands of dinners,
have learned to look at the meal before me
and come home.

Instead of escaping to distant lands,
I've journeyed deep within.
I have become root crop,
a potato sprouting eyes in the dark,
a soul that sees the ripe, yes,
in each moment,
this place, this body,
what these—yes, these!—hands touch.

This onion, creamy white pearl made from mud,
is a tear inside a tear inside a tear,
and, yes,
a many-tiered heart, which changes,
grows like a pearl in me
and, yes,
this garlic smells like sweaty sex
and, yes,
this celery feeds me
salt of the earth.

Blessing for a Midday, Midlife Meal

Life is a clear glass full of sunlight.
Filled with orange juice, wine, water,
it is still full of sunlight.

Life is bread, warm from the oven,
a slice behind and a slice before us.

Life is a glass. You and I are the juice.

Life is bread. You and I are the butter
melting into life's pores.

Life is a cook, and we are life's meat, herbs, spice.

Come hungry to the sunlit kitchen table
set with roses and an ordinary midday meal.

Here we are, raising our glasses,
breaking bread,
this simple moment—
a sacramental feast.

Melting Poem

The buttery smell of baby skin,
potato soup upon the stove—
if I say to you such sensual words—
clicks of heels on wooden stairs,
a long day's rain to melt the snow—

I also say that we are close.
My need to love will let you in,
each moment a greeting in which to dwell,
the ache of open-hearted life,
each gesture's touch, each joining us.

Watercolors painted at dusk,
the foggy earth of changing seasons—
in these you live; I live here, too.
Moss and stone, water and wind.
A frozen lake discovering thaw.

A deep breath in, a slow breath out.
I live in these; I live in you.

The Grain of Salt in the Soup

I love you now, *Beloved*,
like a grain of salt
dissolving in broth,
like a grain of salt
in a kettle where
water and sky,
beans and garlic,
spices and galaxies
are all simmering,
melding together,
melting into the
the stew of stews,
the star-salted universe,
my flavor joining
all flavors brewing
the whole of you.

This love softens me
out of aloneness
into belonging.
I am salt, sea, sun,
and you are the cook
stirring this broth.

Cook me, stir me in,
swirl me out,
and melt me
until I am so lost in you
that salt and kettle are one,
are no-thing,
without limit or scale,
only melting, spinning, falling
into this most nourishing love of all.

Writing and Storytelling

Short Blessings for Poets

1.

May you always
hear the world speaking,
may you listen and respond deeply
and listen again and offer
an even more loving reply,
and may you always have courage
for this life-changing conversation.

2.

May you always
be a child learning to speak,
putting words into your mouth
and tasting for the first time
this wet, old, green world
and its future, brewing.

3.

May you always
hear God, poet of few words,
singing, over and over
in life-begetting joy:

And, yes! let us be—

and, yes! let us be!

Sacred Words in Sacred Places

Let's gather the most sacred words
and write them in sacred places:

heal, give, share—
on pebbles scattered
on our paths;

hearth, earth, art—
in sandstone caves
and sun-warmed canyons;

live, love, now, we—
on all our hands
reaching out to touch;

belonging—
deep inside every cell;

home, welcome, yes—
on the leaves of this tree growing
where I, where you, were born.

Song

Poetry has brought me
to the edge
of speech,
where words
grow so few,
I fall into
the deep well
of silence.

Here, I sit
listening
to presence.
I see,
in the dark,
my path.

I follow its thread
to the place between
ground nothing disturbs
and all I once knew.

Here, I begin to sing.

Meditation on the Word *Through*

"Everything flows, nothing stands still." —*Heraclitus*

Through the keyhole, the wormhole, the grapevine
through the looking glass, the hourglass, the roof
through static, fog, wilderness
cutting through, breaking through
the wind through the open window
the sea through churning rocks
thread through the silver needle
coins through hungry fingers
water through a sieve

through the tunnel, the trees, the maze
through the gap, the straits, the desert
through fire, flames, time
passing through, piercing through
a thief through the city streets
tourists through the gift shop
blood through veins and capillaries
rain through garden soil
tears through tear ducts

through the back door, the gate, the alley
through the heart, the lungs, the ages
through storms, dangers, seasons
flowing through, coursing through
a thunderstorm through a gutter
a stream through a forest

a road through a mountain pass
sound through the air
a bird through a cloudless sky

through the night, the dark, the soil
through the roots, the throat, the center
through a miracle, the eyes of, the auspices of
wandering through, waltzing through
breath through a flute
light through space from a distant star
a wound's sour drainage through bandages
wisdom through the awful grace of God
all things through all things
through and through

Why I Write Poetry

This line must break
because my heart
is breaking,
and in the breaking
is not closing shut
but opening out,
and just as I thought
I was finally making
my life
turn out exactly
the way I
wanted it to go,

life cuts me off
at the pass,
sending me in
the direction I most
fear to go,
and here, now, in this
time, this place
of unexpected change,

I—surprise—
begin to live
and feel more
and feel love
and can't believe
what a fool I was
and what a fool I am,

and my heart is singing—
Yes! break me again!
Break me open,
break me, oh!
Break me, oh!
Break me open.

Each Time I Tell My Story

Each time I tell my story, it is different,
seen through the many ways
of being human.

And there is a listening spirit,
God of many names,
who hears and responds,
and my story becomes
one complicated human story
multiplied by
all my experience of God.

And you, my fellow human,
are also listening,
and you hear and respond
with the stories of your many human ways,
and now, between the three of us—
you, me, and God—
there are at least a million ways of connecting,
a million stories,
love and struggle stories,
which God hears, resoundingly,
in and through each of us;

and remember, there are you and me
and seven billion other me's and you's,
seven billion of us now alive,
all of us multiplied by God,
my story, your stories, our stories,

a living cosmos of stories
all spun by the great storyteller God,

who has made us each a storyteller
so that we can find ourselves and each other
inside the infinite story
from which we are being breathed.

Carry On, Says a Voice in the Dark

Carry on,
says a voice in the dark,
if possible, all the way
to the forgotten mine
of limestone tears,
cave pearls.

Sometimes, I hear children playing
or the call to prayer; sometimes,
the forest coming back.

It is hard to imagine
how much hope, regret,
fear, hatred, hunger,
pain, and dying
we experience
in this place.

And what makes
our story here
most touching:
we don't want it to end.

Zen and the Art of Writing Memoir

I start to write my life story. I say: my story is worth attention.
Look at how hard I have worked, the people I've helped,
struggles I've had, pain overcome, my sacrificing, doing
without. The world is better because of me.

I write about childhood, parents, loves, losses, beliefs, choices.
Surely, the identity I work so hard to claim is more than a
lifeboat, a fortress, a safe armor. Months spent writing. Yet,
who I am or what my life is for eludes me. 20,000 words.
Rereading them bores me.

An inner voice guides, *Cut half. Find what is essential.*

The story grows clearer—10,000 words erased.
Cut half again, the inner voice insists.

At 5,000 words, it's getting interesting. Three, maybe two, core
questions.

Down to 2,000 words, sloughing off skins, dead meaning.
Complex networks of memory distill to essence. The story
shrinks to 500, 300, then 200 words.

Until I admit most has been a long, crazy distraction, asking:
How do I escape suffering?

Which shortens to:
Why do I suffer?

Which shortens to:
Do I suffer?

Laughing inwardly,
something answers,
No!

and begins to live
without the *I*,
each footstep,

each breath

waking.

Prayer of the Local Poet

Yes, there will be a time
when I am gone,
and gone are most
who knew and loved my poems,
my books left yellowing
on dusty corners of shelves
of descendants too busy to read them,
and a few copies, long out of print,
at secondhand bookstores,
where other local poets
occasionally flip through them.

This no longer scares me—
this ceasing to be a poet,
this melting into life's making,
into *poiesis*.

At last, I will *be* poetry!

Sitting

Morning Things

his snoring
rain and distant thunder
forgotten dreams

opening the bedroom door
so quietly
that his snoring rhythm
does not alter

the cat meowing
and clawing the old couch

filling her empty food dish
taking her in my lap
interspecies snuggling and conversation

journal and cup of tea
sun rising behind gray sky
glad for the quiet rain
the wet morning
robin song

solitude
keeping company with
the self that only exists
when no other person or thing
needs anything from me

closing the familiar divide
between longing heart
and burdened mind

alone
becoming one
all one

Sitting in My Car in a Rural Indiana Parking Lot

Wet wind,
chain striking flagpole,
a lakeshore sound,
here among rain clouds
over newly planted Midwest fields
and flowering crabapples.

White petals falling like snow.
This, the season of both.
Between storms,
robins build a nest on an agitated bough.
A dory in a gale.
The shore unseen.
Each moment, a small wave
riding another wave.
Departing as it arrives.
Arriving as it departs.

Sleepy Sitting Practice

Today, no great awakening.
I napped,
the cranky child,
the weary woman,
on a crowded flight,
my head nodding accidentally
onto your shoulder,
Beloved.

You let it stay there.
You let me rest.

Finally, I See

It is not the self
I loathed
but all the stories
I tell and repeat
ad nauseam
about self.

Even the loathing
is just another story
of dislike
and failed conjuring.
False, boring.

Let these stories go.
Freedom!
Self is actually
quiet, empty, loving.

*Gate, gate, paragate, parasamgate**
Is this the liberation you teach?

*Buddhist·mantra from the Heart Sutra. Translated: gone, gone,
gone beyond, gone utterly beyond.

Glimpsed

Breathing, settling into ground,
letting go the hard shell,
the tension fading
until all is soft
within, without.

In the center
of inward vision,
an eye opens, Earth-blue
with long lashes
that touch everything,
an eye that belongs
to all people, all animals,
water, rock, leaf, and star.

Meeting its gaze within, without,
this great eye opens
beyond seeing
into the place where there is
nothing more to see,
and in this moment,
seer and seen are one.

Where to Begin

Yes, there is too much hate.
Near, far, so many people
fighting each other.

And in *my* heart?

Not just a seed,
a full-grown weed
camouflaged
within a righteous garden
of white flowers,
fiery flowers,
conviction,
feels-so-good zeal,
unquestioned.

The inner root grows deepest,
is hardest to see,
and is unbearably painful to pull

with my own loving hands
from my own frightened chest.

Still Learning to Relate

Today, I sit here,
holding a rock, remembering
the distant mountain it came from,
the young man I loved there,

and all the years I struggled,
seeking love in other men,
learning to look within my heart
for you, *Beloved*,
often losing my way.

Well, today, I see that
everything I own
is a relic of the past
and a memento of you.

This house is a temporary museum
of permanent change.

And this mind is a puttering archivist,
a squirrel digging for hidden acorns to chew on,
for memories and old, familiar stories.

Again and again, I've tried to find you
by remembering how I found you before,
as if memories are maps to bliss.

But you never arrive the same way twice.
You are not a story that can be repeated.
I can only meet you in this moment.

"Yes!" you say, kindly, gently,
as you come and sit beside me,

a patient lifelong friend
whom I've never before seen
as my patient lifelong friend.

Reprieve

In just this short meditation,
my mind is spinning
tiny ideas into heroic-scale projects,
each requiring me to leave
what I am already doing
and become an entirely different me,
an extroverted, self-promoting world traveler.

Tomorrow's meditation
and the next day's and the next
will bring more such schemes,
each different, each alluring.

As a young artist,
I saw these bursts of fantasy
as gifts given so that I could—should —
strive for them someday—
divine inspiration calling to me.

As I got older,
I saw myself as failure,
once full of potential but come to nothing,
a neglector of these grand plans,
a flop who started out strong
but never lived up to the ideal.

Today, for the first time,
I simply counted them—
three so far—
and began to ask:
Failing? Or learning?
Learning to sense the difference
between ego's fruitless striving
and being quickened by holy fire?

And as soon as this question woke,
the scaffolding my mind was building
collapsed. Silence returned,
a reprieve given,
and I now rest, embers glowing,
feeling guided, warmed, loved.

Storm

I reach out, *Beloved,*
and feel you
inside,

electricity
in bone

and all around,
far away and close,
waves washing over,
rolling through
this breathed,
embracing air.

I am on fire
and waking
inside thunder.

February

Light, wet snow.
Quiet, slow.

A day with nowhere to go.
A new song on the harp,
then sitting,
looking out the window.

My longed-for simpler life
is here, now, given.

Yes, there are many things
I could turn toward
to fill the day with
cluttered strife.

The old familiar
to-do, to-have, to-hold.

But bold, I do not choose them.

I stay still and breathe.
I rest.
In rest, I find zest.

Light, wet snow.
Quiet, slow,
nowhere to go.

In the Shed

Today, I come to you, *Beloved*,
needing to wail like a train
carrying its heavy load,
a creature exiled from the castle,
living in a shed
through winter and cold, pouring rain.

It feels impossible to come home
to the place of belonging
and beautiful music deep within.
I can only give you tears
of grief and frustration.

And you step in very close
and gently, patiently
massage my tense shoulders,
stroke the headache from my scalp,
lean into my heartache,
and stay with me.

Before I find even a shred
of kindness for myself,
you've got my back.

Dialogue Between Human and God

(parts interchangeable)

Will you?
    Yes.

Can you?
    Yes.

Have you?
    Yes.

Are you?
    Yes.

For you?
    Yes.

Call and Response

Call:
I cannot live
this life without you,
without you.

Response:
Then live
this life without me
within me.

You've been in my body
longer than you've been in your body.
I am the love you left home seeking,
the lover who soul-swallows you whole.

Dancing and Dreaming

Dance, Breathe, Dance

Standing in a doorway, being,
we woke one morning to see
ripe fruit and tender leaves
and heard the murmur of paws
and the whistle of wind
and the heart echoing like a cello
with the loss that churns inside.

Empty and ripe, having come
to the doorstep of compassion,
we trusted its music, its song,
its vibration, and danced
with fleeting summer.

Dance, breathe, dance.
Hang strips of cloth on a wishing tree.

We can become
a tumbling pebble,
a small planet.

We can become
space in the stone,

a softened heart
of many mansions.

In a Hermitage at St. Mary of the Woods
on a Snowy Day

I am dancing,
and from a wooden crucifix on the wall,
a beautifully carved Christ
watches my drumming feet,
my circling with arms opened wide
in thanksgiving,
my blood and flesh
turning to bread and wine,
eucharisteo,*
born from this belly,
these hips,
this pelvis,
this laughing body—
I am dancing with you, *Beloved*!

eucharisteo—grace, joy, thanksgiving, communion

Dance Chant

I am a woman who dances.
I am a dance of a woman.
I am a dance of the Dance.

I am a woman who dreams.
I am a dream of a woman.
I am a dream of the Dreamer.

I am a woman who sings.
I am a song of a woman.
I am a song in the Song.

I am a woman with a story.
I am a story of a woman.
I am a story in the Story.

I am a woman who loves.
I am the love of a woman.
I am love inside Love.

Dervish

Today, I am a young girl
in her new flowing circle skirt,
spinning, arms wide,
laughing to feel her body
spinning with all the sky
and all the earth.

And you, *Beloved,* are the spinning
and everything that spins
and tumbles, turns and flows.

I am the young girl
dancing like a whirling dervish
without even knowing
what a whirling dervish is.

And you are the hawk, soaring on a thermal,
an old stone washed in a stream,
born from fire and ice, being rounded
by your own constant flow.

I am an aging woman,
looking for a still point
in this time when the human world
is dizzily changing,
and people feel lost and afraid.

And you are the turner of the world,
the inciter of the Great Turning,
from dying age to renaissance,
and you need me not to resist,
to join you in building momentum.

I am the girl spinning in her new skirt,
and I am the aging woman,
and still I am surprised,
laughing, crying, needing to dance
for the rest of this life
and beyond with you.

"God Enters Through the Wound" (C. G. Jung)

(This poem came in a dream.)

The wound is here before the injury.

The healing is here before the wound.

The healing creates the wound,

which desires the injury

so that we can learn

to participate

with the healing.

Dreamed at the Beginning of an Ending

The only question on a long and difficult test:

> *The freshly buried corpse speaks.*
> *What does it say?*

The answer:

> *Is. Was. Will be.*
> *The pattern is eternal.*
> *Is dissolving.*
> *I am becoming less than I was.*
> *And more.*

A Dreamed Koan

The frustrated teacher insists:
There are only two choices:
surface and depth.
For the life of the soul,
you must always choose depth.

The scared student argues:
Not always!
And then, without knowing it,
says even more
by falling silent .
and taking a breath.

Dream Girl

Often, at night, in my dreams,
I am with a female companion
who is daughter, mother, friend,
wise girl who knows me by heart.

We walk, swim, talk, laugh, cry together.
She sings to me, tugs my hand, teases,
reminds, heals, urges me to open, open!

She watches me make choices the way
I habitually make choices, and she helps me
fix things when my choices turn out
more stressful and painful than I can handle.

And when I wake up, I sometimes
remember her words, gestures, the dance
we've done, but often, like this morning,
I can't hold on; she flies away beyond all reach,

and all day I miss her and need her,
and at day's end, I climb into bed, hoping
she will find me again and still choose to be
with forgetful, lonely, lost-without-her me.

Petal Moon

Everything is blooming,
flowering, and leafing,
and in the middle of the night,
I open, becoming a dream
of a thousand and more petals,
as many branches
and as many roots,
a dream which blows away
from the sky of my mind
as soon as I wake
yet stays rooted
in the earth of my body
so that this dawn,
as I leave for work,
I know that the world
is imagining my body,
and the universe
is imagining the world,
and I know that the full moon
above the flowering cherry tree
is an exquisite petal,
blown skyward
in one continuous dream.

Healing

Medicine, Mirror, Mother

May you know by heart
the steps to walk
down the aisle to soul.

May you taste everything—
river water, eros, thought,
sand, breath, moss,
oatmeal cookies,
and spiritual practice—

as medicine, mirror, mother
bringing you to life,
showing you
what is sacred,
what spirit is made of,
what is worth living for,
what is worth dying for,
and how everything is holding you.

May you always hear
the harp-calm resonance
at the heart of this journey,
assuring you that this long
wayfaring toward home
is really necessary.

Life, Death

Both require imagination.
Be sure you give some bread to the river,
to people living, mouths to the ground.

The heavy silence of loss
flows in every direction,
north, east, south, and west.

It's a song, a spiral
like a nautilus shell,
and in the soul,
a land largely unknown,
which understands
all is akin to God.

The mountain floats on a lake.
Through you, wild waters pour.

Lunch with Christine

Two introverts, we meet occasionally
for lunch or a hike
when the hepatica are blooming.

Years pass without a word
being said or written between us.

Then, somehow, here we are
over bowls of soup, talking
about what we've contemplated
since we last met:

how I have learned
compassion is not in me
as a personality trait I possess
but is a huge sky,
a bottomless well
not finished birthing any of us;

how she has felt herself sitting
powerless beside another's pain,
and in the dark void sensed
stars and a pulse,
and both her and the other,
so human, being held, healed;

how she has found the simplest words
for life's only requirement:

May I love Love
and let Love
love through me.

And now, bowls empty,
we hug and go our separate ways,

having shared enough
to be fed for years.

Decrescendo

—after "Clearing" by Martha Postlethwaite

Even though you know
how to give yourself to this world,

and the song of your life
has carried you into kitchens, classrooms,
hospitals, and battlefields
full of dissonance, resonance,
and moments of harmony,

this song of yours keeps growing, changing,

and sometimes, the world's suffering
will drown it out,
and your heart becomes
the frantically plucked harp, unheard
beneath the cacophonous orchestra.

And so, a retreat—
into solitude's quiet clearing—
is welcome, is needed.
The trees will take you in,
and the deer, coming at dusk to your path,
will silently bow.

The most essential thing now
is to learn your song's new measures,
its gradual shift
from rhythms of alarm and fury
to contemplation's modal pulse.

Listen. Grieve. Rest. Heal.

Our war-weary world
now needs
especially this
from you.

Laughter

Taken by surprise,
spilling out from the place
shouts and moans come from,
the core muscles around the belly button
bouncing, releasing, and contracting,
an unplanned birthing.

Seconds ago, we were silent,
and then something fluttered in the belly
and is now plunging out of our mouths
to take its first breath—

a hungry baby, who is
born without pain,
lives only for fleeting seconds,
will never need a diaper change,

and leaves us,
not older with grief,
but younger, playful,
childlike again.

The Deep Breath

And isn't it indescribably healing
that the soul does not
forget how to breathe
and decades later
can start its long inhale
and powerful exhale,
giving voice to a lifetime
of wails and words,
now that the body,
long numbed by trauma,
is finally loved enough
to fight free
from the old weight
and see the cruel burden
for what it was?

We Are All on a Boat

and the storm is growing,
and some of us are sunbathing,
and some of us are looking for umbrellas,
and some of us are fighting,
and some of us are taking the boat apart,
and some of us are selling these scraps of wood,
and some of us are making fascinating trinkets from it,
and some of us are hypnotized by these trinkets,
and some of us have claimed the best spaces, the best lounge chairs,
and some of us are crowded down, cramped and hungry,
and some of us are pushing the hungriest ones off the boat,
and some of us are pulling them back on board,
and some of us are sharing space and food with them,
and some of us are watching them drown,
and some of us are repairing the holes,
and some of us are bailing out the sea as it pours in,
and some of us are trying to turn the slow-turning ship,
and some of us are not letting them,
and we all know where greed and hate leads,
and some of us are weary of receiving and inflicting it,
and some of us are learning, listening, caring,
and the storm is the biggest storm ever,
and it is all around us,
and we are on a boat,
sinking with the weight of greed and hate,
rising where love is given,
and there is only one boat.

Three Healing Aphorisms

On Suffering
God *must* suffer *with* us.
Otherwise, God is insufferable.

Penitentiary
Every prison holds someone
we would fight to set free.

Why Butterflies Drink Turtle Tears
The unceasing flow
of ancient salty tears
is needed nourishment
for those who transform.

Columns and Echoes

(read both down and across)

to know	to know	to know	to know
how it is	how it is	how it is	how it is
to be born,	to live,	to be free,	to die,
give birth	change	welcome	love
	and endure	loss	as what is
		now	leaving
			is leaving

Changing Pantoum

Free one thing, everything will change—
hidden weft loosed, just one pulled thread,
ground shifting, a surge of danger,
the bone engraved by hope and dread.

Weft, under, over, thread through thread,
to universe each small thing's hitched,
as is bone to grave, hope to dread,
in cloth that ravels while being stitched.

Flea to star, cosmos to tear hitched,
and every joined thing is moving,
unraveling while being stitched,
changing, dancing, dying, living.

Where everything is joined and moving,
we want to last what can't be stilled,
to change death, time, dance, all living,
into fixed-self, from impermanence distilled.

We want to last. Time won't be stilled.
We try to grab. We try to cling.
Impermanence is self, unstilled.
We cling, but soul lets go and sings.

We fail to grab. We cannot cling.
And so, we learn there is no I.
We release, and letting go, we sing.
No I. No thing. Abide alive.

There is no I. Here is our learning:
old self a stranger, ground shifting
from I as thing to life's boundless yearning—
everything's changed, freed into one-ing!

Healing Story

Long ago, in the wild place
between the sun and moon,
a girl becoming woman
lay crying.

And the one she had hurt,
who had also hurt her,
sat stonily, watching
inside the temporary shelter
they had built.

She spilled open, but he closed off.
She left clad in dirty pain,
shame's curse.

Now, after all this time,
grieving again,
a long series of hurts,
imagination guiding instinctually,
she falls through time
into the eye of the heart

and comes again to that wild place
between sun and moon
and no longer looks for shelter.

And so, at last, she hears
a voice of forgiveness:
This is where it began,
and this is where it ends.

A speaking within,
a fierce knowing
she can't name but trusts.

She lays down the past
and all her failures,
a sacred bundle
on a stone altar,

and back in the present,
she stands, alive in this world,
old and naked and clean.

Beggar

All this time
I've been shopping
the glamor mall
of beautiful
appearances

while you, *Beloved,*
have been waiting
in threadbare rags,
calloused bare feet,
sitting so still
amidst the trash,
the cast-offs, the discarded,

watching,
quietly supplicating,
"Join me! Join me!"

Living Love Poem

First, I was the newborn,
porously alive without a self,
and you were everything I was sensing,
you, the whole world, all new.

Then I was a strange, new world,
a place to be discovered,
and you were the selfless newborn
waking in me.

Then I was afraid to enter you,
the mysterious, all-surrounding forest,
and I was also a tiny, white, spring flower
sheltered against the old oak of your heart.

So, I became a tree,
each year another ring of growth
pulsed from my heart,
and you became the inner whisper,
the nodding trillium,
drawing me in to kneel
at the still point, listening.

There, I became the whisper
and you the pulse,
warm and steady beside my throat.

And I became a wild rose,
flesh flushed, blood warm,
and you the ground
where my petals fell.

And now I am the layered composite earth
softened by cycles of breath and death,
and you are the wild rose,
pricking me to remember
that this losing and finding
is why the world and love were made.

And you are the pouring rain,
the earth-softening rain,
wine of creation,
and I am the cloud,
letting you go.

And you are the storm,
weeping, weeping,
and I am one of your generous tears,
dissolving, dissolving.

I am the dark, the night,
a long winter night,
and you are the firefly,
calling inside me.

And you are the dark universe,
full of longing,
and I am the firefly,
the tiny light,
living star,
sun spark
dancing in you.

You are a poem which has no end.
I've stopped writing
and started living you.

I am a poem which has no end.
You've stopped writing
and started living me.

World House

Look inside the chapel
that ego's dogma
cannot reach.

Questions without answers
urgently call,
buried deep, inherited.

Night gathers a bountiful crop.

Touch stillness,
deeper than name or form,
within soul's house,
dark springtime, arriving quietly,
the world disenthralled.

Don't hurry to turn the lights on.

Here is the candlelight
of wildflowers,

the ancient faith
of newly thawing earth,

the first tremulous wisdom
of a field that has rested.

Our survival,
our feasting,
our oneness

depends on
what this innermost
world house
holds.

All we need
is here.

Five Songs of Compassion

1.

This morning,
the clouds are feathers
lightly brushing against
the bubble of the sky.

And the Earth,
encircled in air,
is a thought,
wafted gently on its way,
in the busy mind of God,
who, deep in meditation,
is letting go all attachment.

2.

And God, breathing in, breathing out,
observes God's busy mind:
rampant galactic musings,
in one inhale dreaming up billions of stars,
and oh, how easy it is
to imagine life beginning,

in a moment of creative distraction,
to pull a planet
just close enough
to a sun
to see what one
yeasty breath across
its waters and its clay
now begets.

3.
How long ago,
enlightened Cosmos,
did you realize
that your own life
is wild
and uncontrollable,

that you seethe, burn, rage, churn,
hurtle, and hurt, riven
with broiling suns
and hurricane galaxies,

that you must feel everything,
your oceans grinding rock to sand,
your every tender cell dividing,

and that we blame you for our human pain
but never even consider yours?

4.

To this, God answers:
If I, with a God-size ego,
were to try ending our shared suffering
by controlling every little thing,
creating the perfection that you beg me for,

wild, painful life
would become a numbing hell
of prisons and tombs,
and I would be hell's dictator.

And so, from birth,
I free you into suffering.

I set you loose in the wild,
on a molten rock
of hungry jungle and labile sea,

knowing that compassion
is the only response,

longing for you to learn this, too,

breathing in all your cries of pain,
all fear, all rage and confusion,

and breathing out
spaciousness,
freedom,
release!

5.

And this explains, dear God,
the dream that you dreamed
in me this winter:

I was cold and afraid and ill,
and a king came and spooned me
with his body,
taking my sickness into him,
absorbing my grief, dying
and melting as healing balm
into my love-thirsty pores.

I woke aglow with this king
coming to life inside me.

And I finally feel,
from inside out,
the compassion Buddhists give
when practicing Tonglen.*

And I finally feel,
from inside out,
the love Christians feel
when reborn as Christ.

*a meditation practice of visualizing taking in another's suffering
on the inbreath and sending out compassion on the outbreath

The Waking Season

Turtles emerge from underwater burrows.
Frogs sing love songs.
Hepatica and twinleaf bloom on north-facing hills.
Oaks and maples, no longer naked,
tassel their many arms and fingers
with green and red pollen-beaded catkins.

We've lived hunkered down in winter,
survival conditions shaping
who we had to be
and what we tried to escape into.

Like everything else,
let's wake.

We too are fed
by inner sap rising up
from deep down,
where it has been cooking.

This balm is turning
all our clenched wounds
into buds opening in the sun
and all our hidden scars
into fruitful flowers.

Tracking the Healer

To listen to another
who is suffering,
be willing to enter
a wilderness
where neither of you
knows the way.

The sufferer feels lost.
But trust that neither of you
will be lost here
if you both listen closely.

The healer in the soul
is just ahead of you,

leaving footprints,
bending twigs,
painting spirals on boulders,
gathering into cairns
blue and gray stones,
sending dreams, telling stories
the body remembers.

Listen and you will see
the thorniest thickets
becoming untangled.

Listen and you will hear
life's thrumming pulse
in the deepest canyons.

Prayer for Choosing to Soften

At best, we will need therapy
and meditation practice
for the rest of our lives,
and some of us will soften
and begin to heal,
and some will keep resisting,
afraid to be other than
alone behind walls.

And the world goes on
as it always has
and always will,
warring more
wherever we resist,
and warring less
wherever we soften.

Sometimes we feel like fools.
We could be getting drunk
and screwing around
in opulent, burning fortresses
instead of humbly sitting here,
becoming naked.

But the love we seek
needs us to live in the wound,
like maggots cleansing
an open sore of infection,
like bees finding pollen

to make honey,
like mystics waking
in the heart of the cosmic rose,
realizing what we called self
was a simple portal,
a crudely carpentered door
we are quietly passing through,
beyond which compassion is
forever opening.

Alive with Tremulous Grace

We seekers believe it will happen
sooner or later:

a place, a hearth fire,
a way home for what seemed
homeless in us,
an all-encompassing music
that frees our forgotten inner song,
waves of compassion, clearing the heart,
making us fiercely tender.

Oh *Love*, how you lure, invite,
and make us lose for you
everything that isn't real.

Yes! We will walk far away
from our old numb sleep
and return to life as mystics.

Zikr*

Oh God of 99 names,
you've invited,
and so I start to sing
my many human names:
    I am Broken,
    Longing to Belong,
    Homeless,
    Seeking Endlessly,
    Clinging to What Is Known,
    Awfully Cruel,
    Well Defended,
    Hurt and Afraid,
    Lost and Alone,
    Divided.

And as I do,
the you in me
echoes in response:
    I am in You,
    I Include Brokenness,
    I Belong to Longing,
    I Am Always Coming Home,
    a Seeker, a Wayfarer, a Soul-farer,
    Letting Go in Unknowing,
    Full of Awe and Love,
    Vulnerable,
    Healing and Courageous,
    Wondering and One,
    Whole.

*an Islamic practice of remembrance, reciting the names and
    aspects of Allah

Home Song

Blue, green world,
Milky Way,
all our lives in such a place,
in one vast soul
and one brief life,
all our lives in mystery.

Dwell in you,
dwell in me,
all our lives, you've been my pulse,
my living Earth,
my sky, my breath,
all our lives, you've been my heart.

Stars above,
roots beneath,
all our lives longing for life,
the pregnant deep,
the soaring wing,
all our lives longing for love.

Sweet music!
Poetry!
All our lives, I've been your song.
Each heart-sung note,
ripe silences,
all our lives, you've sung in me.

In *this* world,
none other,
all our lives spent growing wise,
learning to love
as we grow old,
all our lives spent growing whole.

Me in you,
you in me,
all our lives becoming song,
becoming world,
becoming love,
all our lives becoming home.

Title Index

W

Z

First Line Index

E

F

G

H

I

T

W

Printed in the USA
CPSIA information can be obtained
at www.ICGtesting.com
CBHW011654210324
5610CB00007B/29